SKOOL GRAFFITI

Also available in Beaver by Peter Eldin

The Complete Practical Joker
Skool for Laughs
The Woolly Jumper Joke Book
The Vampire Joke Book

SKOOL GRAFFITI

Peter Eldin

Illustrations by John Miller
Design by Shelagh McGee

Beaver Books

A Beaver Book

Published by Arrow Books Limited
62-65 Chandos Place, London WC2N 4NW

An imprint of Century Hutchinson Ltd

London Melbourne Sydney Auckland
Johannesburg and agencies
throughout the world

First published 1982
Reprinted 1982, 1984 and 1988 (twice)

© Data Forum Ltd 1982

Printed and bound in Great Britain by
Anchor Brendon Limited, Tiptree, Essex

ISBN 0 09 928910 5

INTRODUCTION

As a writer of books for young people I spend a great deal of my time visiting schools all over the British Isles. One of the things that has impressed me in most schools is their lack of graffiti. The majority of pupils, I am pleased to say, appear to respect their school and do not chisel on the desks, write on the walls, or chalk on the blackboard as the kids in this book do.

I trust that you also have respect for other people's property and that you do not scrawl over walls and furniture. The graffiti in this book is quite amusing, but it ceases to be funny if it is used to vandalize property. So, please enjoy this book but leave the graffiti where it belongs – in the book.

If I have found a lack of graffiti in schools, how have I managed to compile a book on the subject? The answer to that question is simple – I have cheated.

Often when I visit schools I hold a joke-telling contest. More often I manage to chat to the pupils and swap jokes. It is from these contests and conversations that the graffiti in this book have come. To name everyone who has contributed would fill the book itself, and I can't remember all the names anyway. I will therefore have to be content with thanking all the school pupils I have met over the years, some of whom have given me ideas for this book but all of whom have contributed to my enjoyment of life.

PETER ELDIN

the school football pitch is
under water
BECAUSE THE PLAYERS DRIBBLE TOO MUCH

SCHOOL FOOTBALL IS A GAME
WITH ONE BALL, 22 PLAYERS
AND UP TO 300 REFEREES

the games master put sawdust
on the football pitch to stop the
school team from slipping out of
the league

my art teacher
paints by numbers

my teacher's Bach
is worse than his
Bitehoven

I THINK MY TEACHER IS A CARD PLAYER.
HE SHUFFLES AS HE WALKS

The school cook has been
cooking for twelve years
- she ought to be done
by now

This school is very
difficult to get into

IT'S ALSO VERY DIFFICULT TO GET
OUT OF

My mind is made up.
I'll go to school tomorrow.
unless I change my mind

I'VE ONLY BEEN AT SCHOOL
TWO WEEKS AND I'M
ALREADY THREE MONTHS
BEHIND.

people in glass houses
shouldn't...

PETE RULES

Kubla Khan is an american secret society

Oxygen has eight sides

Mushrooms are shaped like umbrellas because they grow in wet places

accord is a thick piece of string

Cosmetics make you sick
especially lipsick

Atlas was the greatest thief
of all time. He held up
the world.

The dictionary is the
only place where
success comes before
work.

American time is behind
English time because
England was discovered
before America.

An apple a day keeps the teacher at bay

IF WE LEARN BY OUR MISTAKES I MUST BE GETTING A ~~GUD~~ GOOD EDUCATION

Save energy - write slowly

CRIME DOES NOT PAY - BUT THE HOURS ARE GOOD

Paula ♥ Leroy

I am not an infant prodigy
— my parents are idiots
there's nothing wrong with this school
that an atomic bomb wouldn't put right
I THINK MY TEACHER LOVES ME.
HE ALWAYS PUTS KISSES ON MY WORK
X X
PRAKTIS
MAKES
PURFIKT

Water is composed of oxygin and hydrogin. Oxygin is pure but hydrogin is a mixture of gin and water.

People who live in London must be the most idiotic in Britain for that is where the Population is most dense.

Do ghosts believe in people?

Ruddy hard Kipling
writes exceedingly good
books.

THE THUNDER GOD WENT FOR A RIDE

UPON HIS FAVOURITE FILLY

"I'M THOR" HE CRIED

THE HORSE REPLIED

"YOU FORGOT YOUR THADDLE THILLY"

Jonah was the strongest
man in the world. Even
a whale couldn't keep him
down.

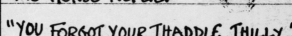

CABBIDGE

IF YOU WANT HIGHER EDUCATION SIT ON A STEPLADDER IN CLASS
Education is a wonderful thing - it's wasted on children
DRAOBKCALBSIHT DNIHEB DEPPART 'I PLEH
I'm as clever as the next person - too bad he's an idiot

Our headmaster is boss-eyed, he can't control his pupils

THE SKULL OF
ROBIN HOOD

THE SKULL OF
ROBIN HOOD
AS A
YOUNG BOY

DO
RED CORPUSCLES
LIVE IN VEIN?

Billy
=
Sarah

A MAN FELL DOWN A SEWER
AND IN THE SEWER HE DIED
THE JUDGE GAVE HIS VERDIC
HE SAID IT WAS SEWERCIDE

our school has automatic
central heating - every time
the weather gets cold it
automatically breaks down

MUFC

AL=
vi

oes a cow with hiccoughs
hurn its own butter?

BE GENEROUS - IF YOU'VE
OT MEASLES GIVE THEM
EVERYONE IN THE SCHOOL

n't worry if your job is small
d your rewards are few
member that the mighty oak
as once a nut like you

E OPEN MINDED -
BLOW YOUR BRAINS OUT

HELP!

AMY

CUT EDUCATION COSTS
SHOOT ALL THE TEACHERS
KEEP YOUR SCHOOL TIDY!
throw your rubbish out of the windows
LET'S HAVE A SCHOOL MAGAZINE
and then we can blow up the school
WHERE'S THE SCHOOL SPIRIT?
HE ONLY HAUNTS AT NIGHT
Lost: One science teacher after yesterday's experiment
TEE HEE

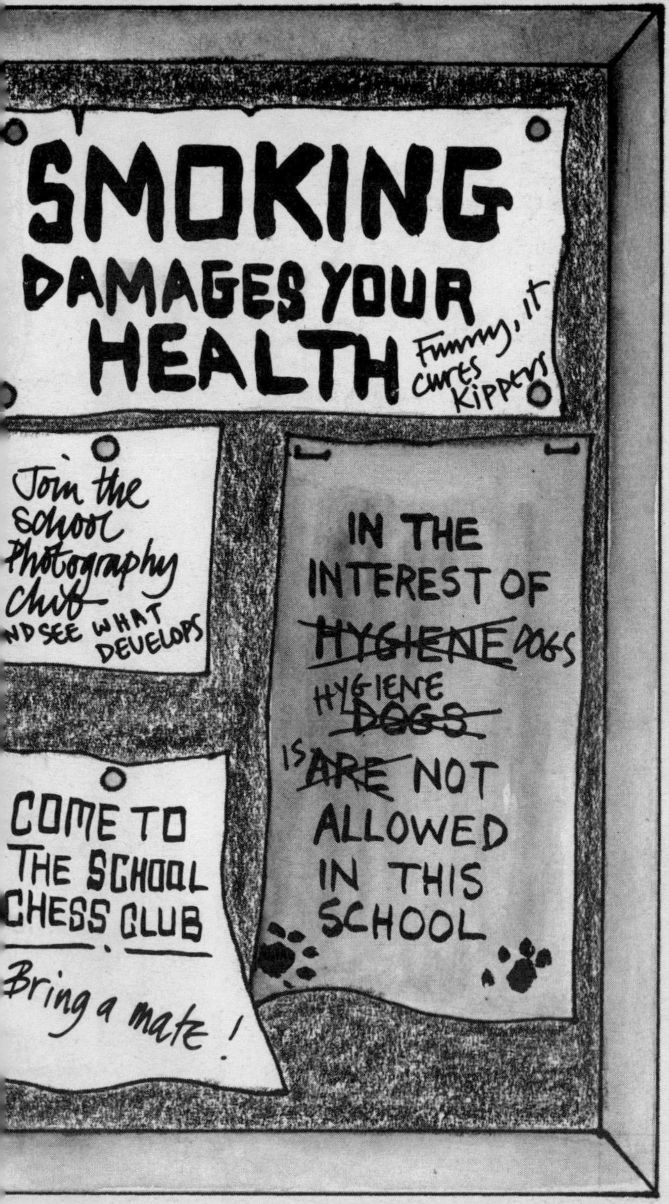

SMOKING DAMAGES YOUR HEALTH
Funny, it cures kippers
Join the school Photography club
ND SEE WHAT DEVELOPS
IN THE INTEREST OF ~~HYGIENE~~ DOGS
HYGIENE ~~DOGS~~
IS ~~ARE~~ NOT ALLOWED IN THIS SCHOOL
COME TO THE SCHOOL CHESS CLUB
Bring a mate!

EVERYONE WRITES
ON WALLS EXCEPT
ME

MARY

my teacher
calls me wonder boy
YES, HE LOOKS AT YOU
AND WONDERS

my father always brings
me to school - we're in
the same class

I USED TO BE CONCEITED
-BUT NOW I'M PERFECT
Signed: Know-all Edmunds

teacher is a square
rubik is a cube
I HATE GRAMMAR
and I don't like Grandad
10x1 =
101
I THINK I MUST
BE TEACHER'S PET
-HE KEEPS ME IN A
CAGE
I like School
when it's closed

LITTLE JACK HORNER SAT
IN A CORNER - B.O.

BE CREATIVE

Create a ted cher
torture

IF BATMAN IS SO CLEVER
WHY DOES HE WEAR HIS
UNDERPANTS OVER HIS
TROUSERS?

WHEN THINGS GET TWISTED AND
OUT OF JO
DON'T GET DISCOURAGED AND QUIT
THE GAM
REMEMBER, A CORKSCREW
NEVER GOES STRAIGHT
TO THE POINT

BUT IT GETS THERE JUST THE SAME

GARY

is won derful blow your mind-
without it yood smok e dy námite

UNIVER RSITY AND BE MOST
DU CATED PERS ON THE DOLE

THUR — IN THE QUEUE
at's the Our s chool is so posh
ars spell WE don't do
weather vulga r fract ions
re had THE ONLY THING
me a long I PASSED IN MY
UR SCHOOL EXAM WAS a RUBBER
so POSH TO MY MA TE
's AN
PPROVED OUR ART CAN'T
CHOOL TEA CHER THE.
EVEN DRAW
CUR TAINS

SCHOOL DRAMATIC
SOCIETY
PROGRAMME

List of characters

Hamlet—a cigar

Ophelia Pulse

Horatio (A HALF NELSON)

Polonius—a spicy sausage

Gravedigger AN OUT OF WORK
HEAD MASTER

Rosencrantz & (BY COURTESY
Guildenstern OF T. STOPPARD)

A red indian's wife is called his
squaw and his children are
called squawkers.

a bird in the hand can make
a horrible mess

If Guy Fawkes had succeeded
in blowing up Parliament
the house would have
risen sooner than
expected.

The wife of a sultan is
called a sultana.

It stands to raison

The French national anthem is
the Mayonnaise

I do not know the speed of light
but it must be very fast. It
certainly reaches earth too
early in the morning.

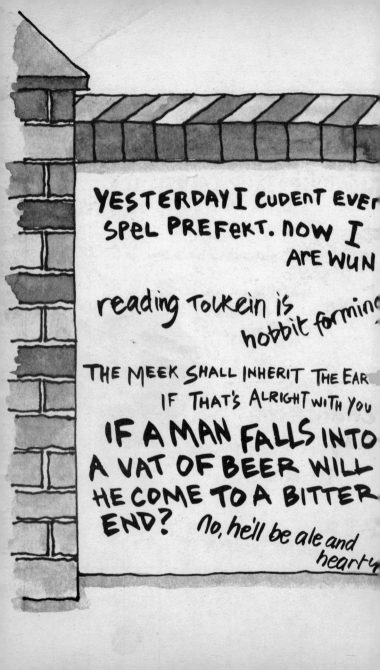

HE MEEK SHALL INHIBIT THE EARTH
are there any intelligent pupils in this school?
NO I'M ONLY VISITING
n my boarding school they change the sheets every day. – From one bed to another
P.P.R
CFC

I'm the type of person my mother'd doesn't want me to associate with.

If two's company and three's a crowd what's four and five?

NINE

FAITH CAN MOVE MOUNTAINS

she's a big strong girl

SDRAWKCAB IS
BACKWARDS
SPELT BACKWARDS

mime should
be scene and
not heard

I'd GIVE MY RIGHT ARM
TO BE AMBIDEXTROUS

PUT A DRAWING PIN
ON YOUR TEACHER'S
CHAIR - THAT WILL
KEEP HIM ON HIS TOES

KEEP SMILING - IT
MAKES EVERYONE
WONDER WHAT YOU'RE
UP TO

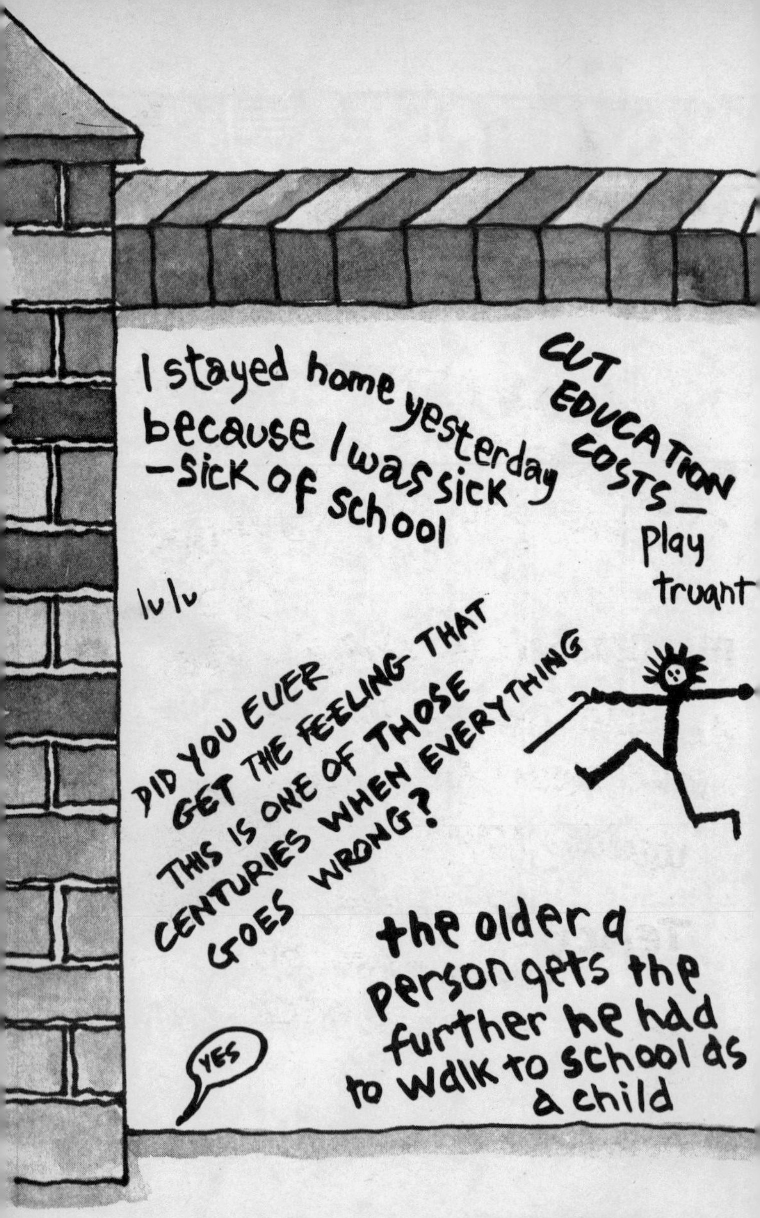
I stayed home yesterday because I was sick -sick of school
CUT EDUCATION COSTS — Play truant
lulu
DID YOU EVER GET THE FEELING THAT THIS IS ONE OF THOSE CENTURIES WHEN EVERYTHING GOES WRONG?
YES
the older a person gets the further he had to walk to school as a child

ADULTS ARE ALWAYS MOANING
—PERHAPS THAT'S WHY THEY
ARE CALLED GROAN-UPS

my teacher is strict — she
deducts marks if you
put your full stops
upside down

TEACHER IS AN
ANAGRAM OF
CHEATER

I DID AND A CAR KNOCKED ME DOWN!

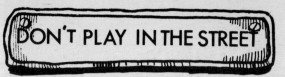

DON'T PLAY IN THE STREET

YOU COULD GET THAT RUN DOWN FEELING

When Marley's ghost appeared
bound in chains Scrooge said:
"Are you a punk?"

Macadam was the first
Scotsman

There are four quartz to the
gallon

Was Buffalo Bill half animal
and half man?

donald duck is quackers

Forever Amber: A story about
a broken traffic light

If a glass blower inhales does
he get a pane in his stomach?

RUBIK'S A SQUARE

The whole world's gone
cubic

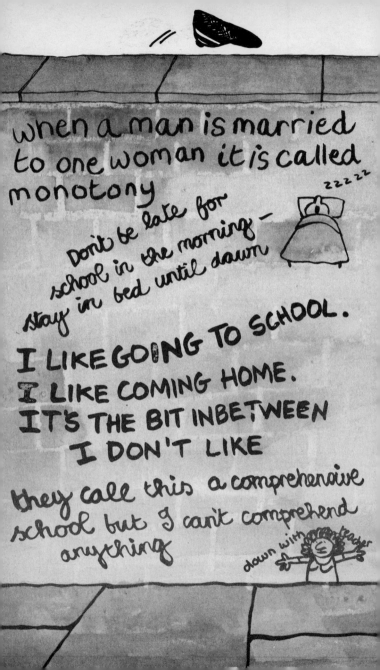

when a man is married to one woman it is called monotony

Don't be late for school in the morning – stay in bed until dawn

I LIKE GOING TO SCHOOL.
I LIKE COMING HOME.
IT'S THE BIT INBETWEEN
I DON'T LIKE

they call this a comprehensive school but I can't comprehend anything

down with teacher

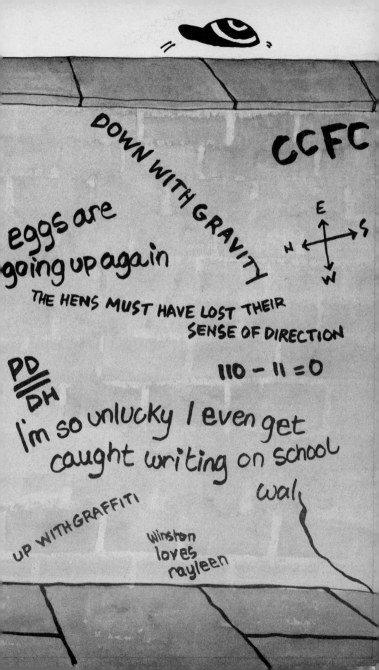

September, November and December are the warmest months of the year because they all have embers in them.

Poetry is when every line starts with a capital letter.

A vacuum is an empty space in which the Pope lives

A gargoyle is used for rinsing your throat when it's sore.

asses are little donkeys

Anyone for Tennyson?

who's the poet lying in the sun?
-ROBERT BROWNING

HOMER WROTE THE ODDITY

EXERCISE KILLS GERMS

Sure, but how do you get the germs to exercise?

He laughed when they said
It couldn't be done
He smiled and said he knew it
But he tried that thing that
couldn't be done
And found he couldn't do it

WE HAVE WAYS OF
MAKING YOU CHALK

SAVE TIME — PUT A CALENDAR
IN YOUR PIGGY BANK

THE ONLY WAY TO AVOID MISTAKES
IS TO GAIN EXPERIENCE
THE ONLY WAY TO GAIN EXPERIENCE
IS TO MAKE MISTAKES

The dictionary
is the only place
where success
comes before
work

NOSTALGIA
ISN'T
WHAT
IT USED
TO BE

IT's easy to become
A Teacher — you
leARn The Job By degrees

MT
MF

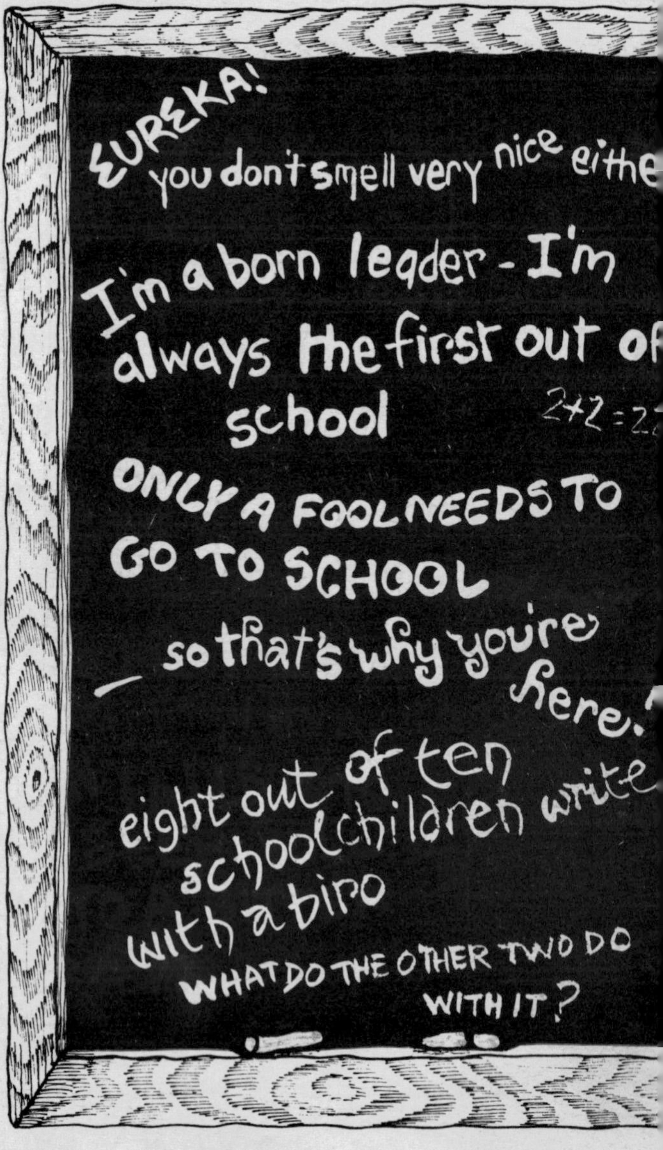
EUREKA!
you don't smell very nice eithe
I'm a born leader - I'm always the first out of school
2+2=2
ONLY A FOOL NEEDS TO GO TO SCHOOL
— so that's why you're here.
eight out of ten schoolchildren write with a biro
WHAT DO THE OTHER TWO DO WITH IT?

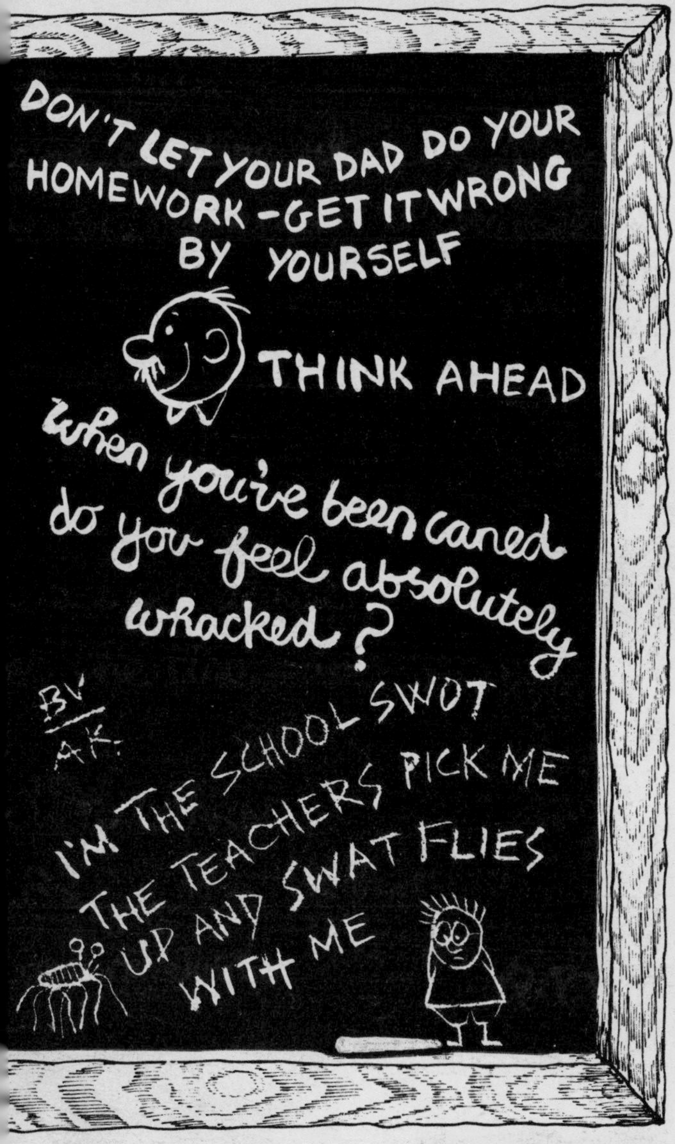

DON'T LET YOUR DAD DO YOUR HOMEWORK - GET IT WRONG BY YOURSELF
THINK AHEAD
when you've been caned do you feel absolutely whacked?
BV / AK.
I'M THE SCHOOL SWOT
THE TEACHERS PICK ME UP AND SWAT FLIES WITH ME

BAN SHEEPDOG TRIALS
- THE DOGS ARE INNOCENT

The money used by Eskimoes is called Iced lolly

BACON DISCOVERED THE MAGNIFYING GLASS - AND AT OUR BOARDING SCHOOL YOU NEED A MAGNIFYING GLASS TO DISCOVER THE BACON

THE POPE IS INNOCENT IV OK?

Examination Rule:

Anyone found cheating will be awarded ten marks for initiative.

Do horses have to take their hay levels?

In every exam I get almost 100% - I get the two ~~nort~~ noughts

GO TO SCHOOL TO LEARN THE THREE Rs

Ravage, riot and revolution

Do gardeners have to study for a dig-ree?

Did Father Christmas have to take his ho ho ho levels?

If you are not confused you have misunderstood the question

Avoid the rush - fail your exams now

Exams are never as easy as they're made out to be

TIP FOR ORAL EXAMS:
WHEN IN DOUBT - MUMBLE

Famous People

Everyone was petrified in the Stone Age.

Samson was the best actor in the Bible — He brought the house down

Sir Cumference was a knight of the round table

Old King Cole was the father of the Black Prince

William the Corn-curer was a famous chiropodist who ruled England.

Socrates died from an overdose of wedlock

Adam must have been the
fastest runner in history. He
was first in the Human Race.

The ruler of Russia was
called the Czar, his wife
was the Czarina and his
children were Czardines.

Philatelists were a race of
people who lived in
biblical times

Please don't blame my doggy
It's not his fault at all
Someone left a wet umbrella
Standing in the hall

Inventors

Fire was invented by
a bright spark

When the wheel was invented it
caused a revolution

robinson Crusoe invented
the five day week for
he had all his work
done by Friday

Fractions were invented by
Henry $\frac{1}{5}$

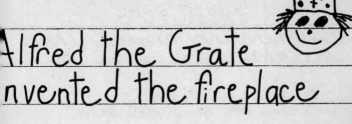

Alfred the Grate
invented the fireplace

~~Robot~~ ROBERT THE
BRUCE WATCHED A
SPIDER CLIMBING UP
AND DOWN AND THEN
he invented tHe yoyo

a ruminating animal chews
its cubs

Dolphins are very intelligent.
within only a few weeks of being
in captivity they can train a
man to stand at the edge of
their pool and throw them
fish three times a day.

Do chickens get people pox?

Can a frog get a person
in its throat?

RDS HAVE A SECOND STOMACH.
IT IS CALLED THE BLIZZARD

The highest form of animal
life is the giraffe.

uckens are the only creatures you can

at before they are born and

after they are dead.

When a bull falls in love
it is for heiffer

Geography notes

Venetians come from Venus

Greece is the Slipperiest
country in the world

Germs come from Germany

THE EQUATOR IS AN IMAGINARY LION
RUNNING ROUND THE EARTH

THE ANDES ARE AT THE
END OF YOUR ARMIES

the eastern part of Asia
is called Euthanasia

People in Finland don't
need to diet - they're
fin enough already

CHILE IS THE COLDEST COUNTRY
IN THE WORLD

RUSSIA IS A VERY FAST PLACE—
ITS PEOPLE ARE ALWAYS RUSSIAN

	Monday	Tuesday
9 am.	FRENCH is all Greek to me	ENGLISH LIT
10 am	ART	CHEMISTRY
10·30 am	Break	Break
11 am	P.T.	GEOGRAPHY
12 pm	Lunch	Lunch
Double	LATIN is a dead language As dead as dead can be	ENGLISH LIT (POETRY) I hate all school subjects but
Lessons	It killed off all the Romans. And now it's killing me	poetry is the verse

Wednesday	Thursday	Friday
MATHS 2+2 = 22	PHYSICS	BIOLOGY
HISTORY Lessons are a thing of the past	LATIN is a dead language - and the teacher's not very	MUSIC lively either
Break	Break	Break
ART	SOCIAL STUDIES	ENGLISH LANG
Lunch	Lunch	Lunch
GEOGRAPHY is the same all over the world	GAMES	HISTORY is the fruitiest lesson because it is full of dates

Biology

We all sprang from monkeys. But some didn't spring far enough.

A colon is a punctuation mark in the human body

" The child is father to the man" was written by Shakespeare. He failed his biology exam.

Blood is composed of red corkscrews and white corkscrews.

The only cure for water on the brain is a tap on the head.

THE APPENDIX IS PART OF A BOOK FOUND IN THE BODY.
Is it near the index finger?

A skeleton is a man with his outsides off and his insides out.

Parenthood is hereditary. If your parents didn't have any children it is likely that you will not have any either.

HISTORY

Wellington was a great soldier who went into battle determined to win or lose.

Charles I was off his head.

The most remarkable achievement of the Romans was learning Latin.

The dark ages were so called because they had lots of Knights

~~SPQR~~   QPR

Samson was a strong man
He could break an iron hoop
But he never could have done it
If he'd had some of our school
soup.

Henry the Eighth had six
wives because he liked to
chop and change

RICHARD COEUR DE LION
WAS THE FIRST HEART
TRANSPLANT PATIENT.

dry your hands thoroughly after washing
IF YOU DON'T YOUR NAILS WILL GO RUSTY
ONLY DIRTY PEOPLE NEED TO WASH
PLEASE WASH YOUR NECK. Signed DRACULA
DRACULA IS A PAIN IN THE NECK
never drink water -if it can rust iron just imagine what it can do to your stomach
PLEASE WASH YOUR HANDS AFTER USING THIS TOWEL

(⊘) MUSH ROOM   ~~death list~~ (⊘)

~~DINING~~ROOM MENU 🪰

Starters: ~~DRACULA'S BLOOD~~
~~Tomato juice, noodle~~
~~soup~~ nourishment for the brain

Main Courses:
~~FRIED BATHMATS~~   ~~DEAD SLUGS IN AXLE GREASE~~
~~Beefburgers & chips,~~
~~STICKS OF DYNAMITE~~   ~~Pulverised~~
~~Sausages & mash,~~ polystyrene

~~DRAINPIPES IN POLYFILLA~~
~~Macaroni cheese~~

~~SOURS~~   ~~tarmac path~~
~~Sweets: Treacle tart,~~

~~tonsils in quicksand~~
~~Plums & custard,~~

~~SOAP ON CARDBOARD~~
~~Cheese & biscuits~~

the graffiti on this menu is bad
SO'S THE FOOD

(⊘)   (⊘)

ask the flies

IF YOU PUT YOUR HANDS IN ALPHABET SOUP ARE YOU GROPING FOR WORDS?

EAT SPINACH AND YOU'LL GROW STRONG ENOUGH TO REFUSE IT

good school meals are made by accident

school dinners are going up

I don't like cabbage and I'm glad I don't like it. If I did like it I'd have to eat it — and I hate the stuff

THEY'RE DIFFICULT TO KEEP DOWN

VENI, VIDI, VOMITI

School dinners are very tasty — I had one last week and I can still taste it

my art teacher is knock-kneed, ugly and stupid
WHAT ARE HER BAD POINTS?
MY ENGLISH TEACHER HAS JUST TURNED 28. BEFORE SHE TURNED IT SHE WAS 82.
MR SQUEERS IS ALIVE AND WELL AND TEACHING AT OUR SCHOOL
what, the dickens!
Art teachers never die – they just draw to a close

IF YOU CAN'T SAY IT TO THE HEADMASTER'S FACE, SAY IT BEHIND HIS BACK

my biology teacher is so strict he caned me for cheating in an exam—he saw me counting my ribs

My French teacher is a redhead—no hair just a red head

SOTHEBY'S ARE SELLING SOME OLD MASTERS NEXT WEEK—PERHAPS THEY'D

Those who can, do.
Those who can't, teach

Our maths teacher counts
on his fingers

80% of headmasters take
'The Times'.

The remaining 20% buy it.

Don't go to school —
sleep at home

My music teacher plays the piano by ear. I prefer to use my fingers.

the trubel with Kids todae is that thae Kant spel Kereckly.

OUR HEADMASTER IS SO OLD HE SQUEAKS WHEN HE TALKS AND CREAKS WHEN HE WALKS

Skule Rools

Twelve inches rule, OK ?

signed: MICHAEL FOOT

Slide rules, √OK ?

DAVID BELLAMY RULES, OAK HAY:

English teacher rules, OK, alright
agree, concede, admit, accept ?

Einstein rules relatively, OK ?
WELL, IN THEORY ANYWAY

James Bond rules OO7

Anagrams lure, OK ?

Scots rule, och, aye ?

Examples rule, e.g.

Wyatt Earp rules, OK corral?

Archimedes rules, EureKay?

Amnesia rules, er... er... er

QUEEN ELIZABETH
   RULES, UK

Queensberry rules, K.O.

OK

When I Leave School

1. I would like to be a fireman because my teacher is always telling me to go to blazes

2. I would like to be the owner of a flea circus – but I would be prepared to start from scratch.

3. I would like to be a mortuary assistant but it's a bit of a dead end job.

4. I would like to be a ~~Which~~ Witch but I can't spell I

5. I would like to be a chimney sweep. because I think the work would soot me.

6. I would like to be a borough surveyor and spend all my time inspecting rabbit holes.

7. I would like to be a hairdresser because there's a lot of fringe benefits.

8 I WOULD LIKE TO BE A MANICURIST AND THEN I'D MAKE MONEY HAND OVER FIST

9. I would like to be a human cannonball because I'm sure I'm of the right calibre

10. I would like to be a doctor because I have such bad handwriting

SCHOOL MEALS SHOULD CARRY A GOVERNMENT HEALTH WARNING

CHOKING

:·NO SMOKING!·:

My uncle is 100
—he owes his
longevity to
school dinners.
He never ate
them.

greens put
colour in your cheeks

**GOBLIN
YOUR FOOD
IS BAD FOR
YOUR ELF**

You can tell our school canteen
is clean. Everything
tastes of soap.

ESPECIALLY THE
BUBBLE AND
SQUEAK

School food makes
you sicker quicker

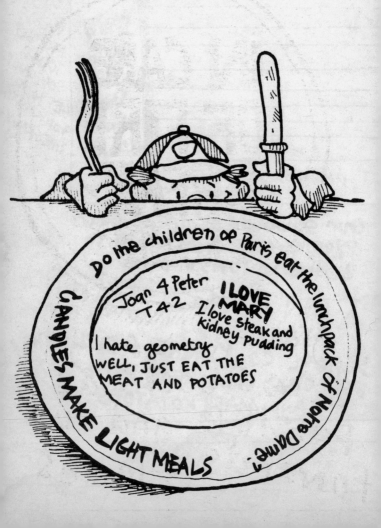

IN CASE
OF FIRE
BREAK
GLASS

grab as many
schoolbooks as
possible and run
towards flames

JOKE BOOKS

Have you heard about all the hilarious joke books published by Beaver? They are available in bookshops or they can be ordered directly from us. Just complete the form below and enclose the right amount of money and the books will be sent to you at home.

☐ THE VAMPIRE JOKE BOOK	Peter Eldin	£1.50
☐ THE WOOLLY JUMPER JOKE BOOK	Peter Eldin	£1.25
☐ THE WOBBLY JELLY JOKE BOOK	Jim Eldridge	£1.50
☐ NOT THE ELEPHANT JOKE BOOK	John Hegarty	£1.50
☐ THE CRAZY CRAZY JOKE BAG	Janet Rogers	£1.95
☐ THE CRAZY JOKE BOOK	Janet Rogers	£1.50
☐ EVEN CRAZIER JOKES	Janet Rogers	£1.50
☐ THE CRAZIEST JOKE BOOK EVER	Janet Rogers	£1.50
☐ THE CRAZY JOKE BOOK STRIKES BACK	Janet Rogers	£1.50
☐ THE ELEPHANT JOKE BOOK	Katie Wales	£1.50
☐ JOKES FROM OUTER SPACE	Katie Wales	£1.25
☐ SANTA'S CHRISTMAS JOKE BOOK	Katie Wales	£1.50

If you would like to order books, please send this form, and the money due to:
ARROW BOOKS, BOOKSERVICE BY POST, PO BOX 29, DOUGLAS, ISLE OF MAN, BRITISH ISLES. Please enclose a cheque or postal order made out to Arrow Books Ltd for the amount due including 30p per book for postage and packing both for orders within the UK and for overseas orders.

NAME . . . .

ADDRESS . . . .

. . . .

Please print clearly.